I0820837

Dumbo Octopus and Other STRANGE Squid and Octopuses

by Rachel Rose

Bearport Books, an imprint of Bearport Publishing by FlutterBee

Credits
Cover and title page, © DiveIvanov/Shutterstock and © imageBROKER/Alamy Stock Photo and © Jeff Rotman/Alamy Stock Photo and © Science History Images/Alamy Stock Photo; 3, © cloud7days/Adobe Stock; 4–5, © Dario Spagnolo/Adobe Stock and © Sam Robertshaw/Shutterstock and © YU YUN–PING/Shutterstock and © GeraldRobertFischer/Adobe Stock and © Mark/Adobe Stock and © Thararat/Adobe Stock; 6, © Chronicle/Alamy Stock Photo; 6–7, © NOAA; 7, © NOAA; 8, © Ross/Tom Stack Assoc/Alamy Stock Photo; 8–9, © ead72/Adobe Stock; 9TR © Mike Veitch/Alamy Stock Photo; 9BL © Jeff Rotman/Alamy Stock Photo; 10, © Teguh Tirtaputra/Shutterstock; 10–11, © Chris Newbert/Minden Pictures; 11TL, © Soonyoung Han/iStock; 11BR, © Izuzuki/Adobe Stock; 12, © Nature Picture Library/Alamy Stock Photo; 12–13, © Blue Planet Archive LLC/Alamy Stock Photo; 13TL, © Sam Robertshaw/Shutterstock; 13BL, © Sam Robertshaw/Shutterstock; 14, © feathercollector/Shutterstock; 14–15, © David Fleetham/Alamy Stock Photo; 15, © Pommeyrol Vincent/Shutterstock; 16, © Masayuki Abe/Nature Production/Minden Pictures; 16–17, © Tony Wu/NPL /Minden Pictures; 17, © Blue Planet Archive LLC/Alamy Stock Photo; 18, © Nikivas/Wikimedia; 18–19, © NOAA Okeanos Explorer Program, Gulf of Mexico 2012 Expedition; 19, © mauritius images GmbH/Alamy Stock Photo; 20, © DiveIvanov/Shutterstock; 20–21, © ZUMA Press, Inc./Alamy Stock Photo; 22, © Sipa USA/Alamy Stock Photo; 23, © YU YUN–PING/Shutterstock

Bearport Publishing Company Product Development Team
Kayla Eggert, Theresa Emminizer, Kim Jones, Allison Juda, Cole Nelson, Naomi Reich, Steve Scheluchin, Tiana Tran

Statement on Usage of Generative Artificial Intelligence
Bearport Publishing remains committed to publishing high-quality nonfiction books. Therefore, we restrict the use of generative AI to ensure accuracy of all text and visual components pertaining to a book's subject. See BearportPublishing.com for details.

Library of Congress Cataloging-in-Publication Data is available at www.loc.gov or upon request from the publisher.

ISBN: 979-8-89577-629-2 (hardcover)
ISBN: 979-8-89577-717-6 (ebook)

For more information, write to Bearport Publishing, 3500 American Blvd W, Suite 150, Bloomington, MN 55431.
Printed in the United States of America.

CONTENTS

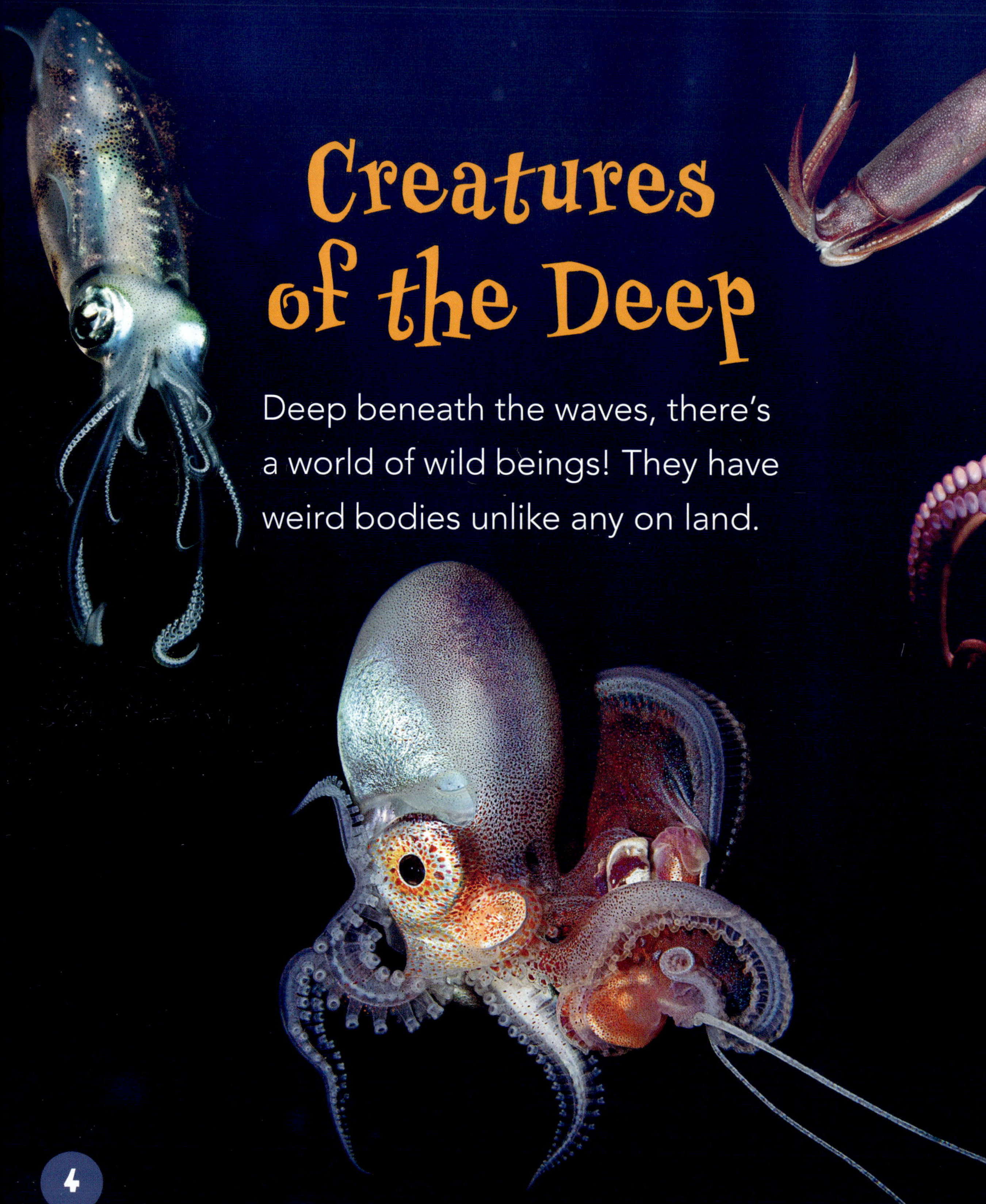

Creatures of the Deep

Deep beneath the waves, there's a world of wild beings! They have weird bodies unlike any on land.

One curious creature has a bell-shaped body with eight arms, three hearts, and no backbone. It's a Dumbo octopus! This creepy cutie is just one of many strange octopuses and squid in the sea. Let's dive in to find more underwater oddities.

Dumbo Octopus

Listen up! A Dumbo octopus may look like it has big ears . . . but these odd body parts are actually large fins. The fins help this octopus swim in the deep waters where it lives 13,000 feet (4,000 m) below sea level. That's deeper down than any other octopus that we know of.

This octopus is named after the big-eared flying elephant in Disney's *Dumbo*.

Dumbos are a kind of umbrella octopus. Their arms are connected by webbing, making them look like umbrellas when spread out.

Dumbo octopuses have very few predators because they live so deep in the sea.

Though they have big fins, Dumbo octopuses have small bodies—measuring about 8 inches (20 cm) long.

Mimic Octopus

Now you see me, now you don't! The mimic octopus is a master of **disguise**. It can change its shape to look like a lionfish, a jellyfish, or even a sea snake. But changing it up isn't for fun and games. The mimic octopus copies these **venomous** creatures to scare away predators.

Mimic octopuses are good at blending in with the sandy seafloor.

Having a squishy body allows the mimic octopus to become all kinds of crazy shapes.
Mimicking a crab
Mimic octopuses were first discovered in 1998. They are so good at hiding that people hadn't known they existed before this!
No other animal is known to shift into as many different forms as a mimic octopus.
Mimicking a sea snake

Blue-Ringed Octopus

Don't be fooled by these small, colorful creatures. Blue-ringed octopuses are among the deadliest animals in Earth's oceans. These drop-dead beauties have enough venom to kill up to 26 people within minutes! Their bright-blue rings appear when predators are close by—warning would-be attackers to stay far away.

Blue-ringed octopuses make their homes in the Pacific and Indian Oceans.

When asleep, these octopuses are usually brown or pale yellow in color.
Blue-ringed octopuses hunt at night. They eat mostly shellfish, such as shrimp and hermit crabs.
The blue-ringed octopus is about the size of a golf ball.

Blanket Octopus

Watch out! The **female** blanket octopus has a secret **defense**. When in danger, she fans out her huge, blanketlike cape! This makes her look bigger and scares away predators. While these impressive females are up to 6 ft. (2 m) long, **male** blanket octopuses are much smaller. Males don't have capes and are only around 1 in. (2.5 cm) long.

The blanket octopus's cape has colorful spots that look like eyes! This helps scare predators.

Eye spots

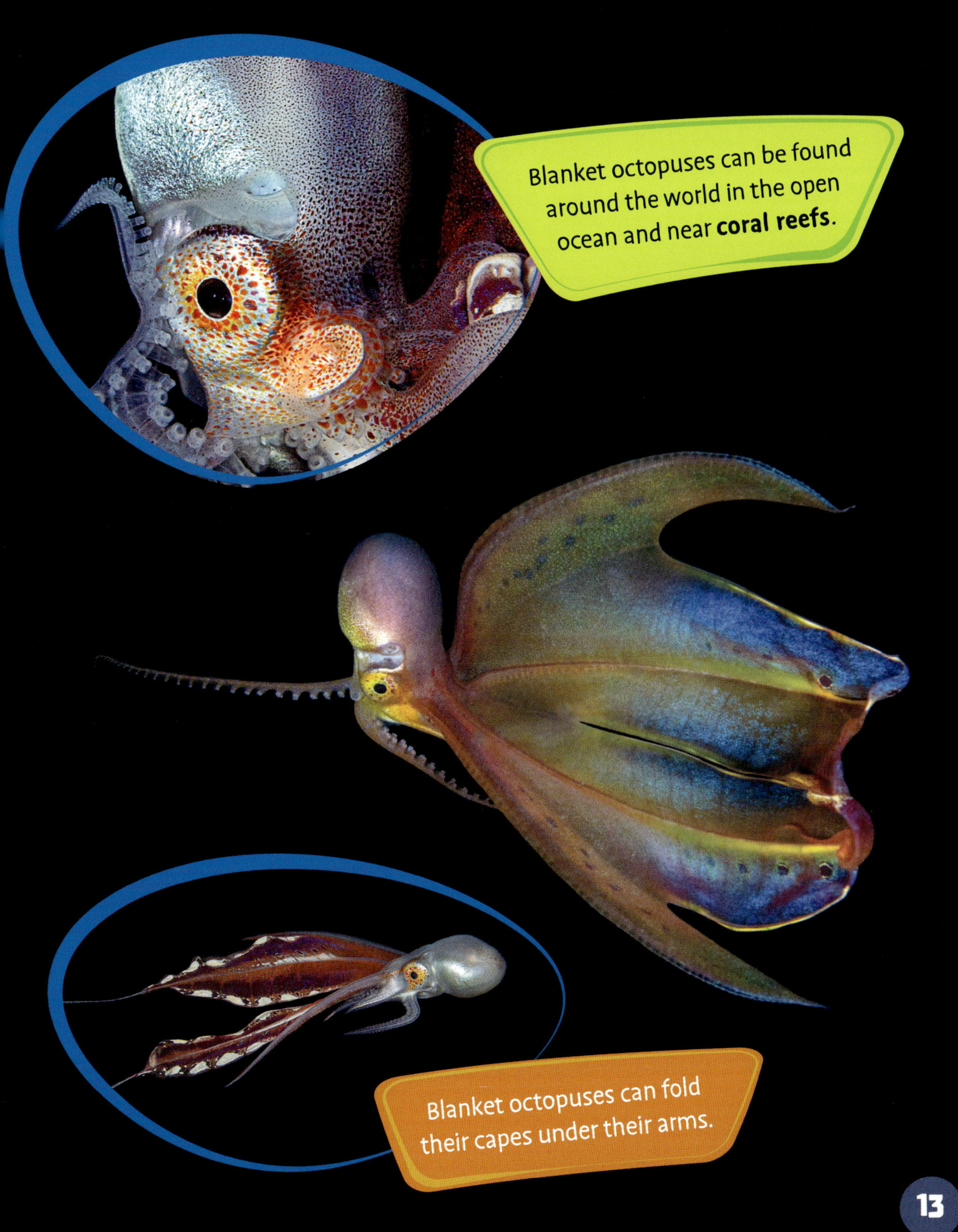

Blanket octopuses can be found around the world in the open ocean and near **coral reefs**.

Blanket octopuses can fold their capes under their arms.

Purpleback Flying Squid

It's a bird! It's a plane! No, it's a purpleback flying squid! This creature doesn't have wings, but it can seem to fly, shooting itself up to 100 ft. (30 m) above the surface of the water. It zips through the air at speeds up to 20 miles per hour (32 kph). This allows the squid to make a quick escape when it's being hunted.

These squid live in the open ocean.

Purpleback flying squid are **prey** to many big fish, including sharks, swordfish, and tuna.

Purpleback flying squid are not picky about what they eat. Often, they make a meal of other squid!

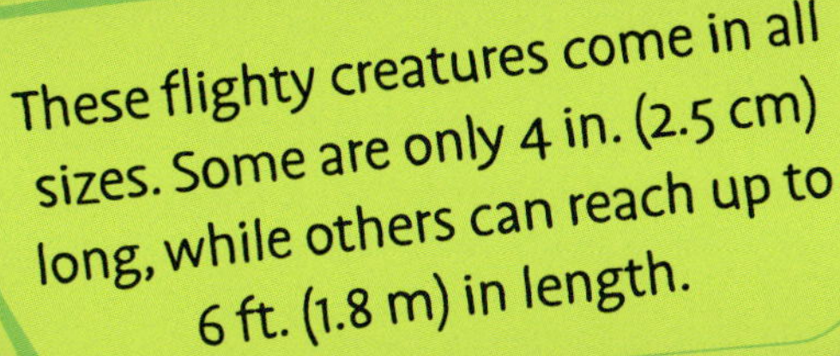

These flighty creatures come in all sizes. Some are only 4 in. (2.5 cm) long, while others can reach up to 6 ft. (1.8 m) in length.

Japanese Pygmy Squid

Meet the smallest squid in the ocean! Male Japanese pygmy squid grow up to only 0.6 in. (1.5 cm) long, while females are around 1 in. (2.5 cm). That's about the length of a paper clip. But don't be fooled by their size. Pygmy squid are good hunters. They can kill shrimp, crabs, and other prey that are bigger than they are.

When it wants to rest or hide, a pygmy squid makes a kind of sticky glue to cover its body. This helps the animal attach itself to seagrass.

Japanese pygmy squid sneak up on their prey, catching them with their tentacles. Then, they bite and **paralyze** the prey with venom.

A Japanese pygmy squid's life is short. Most live fewer than 150 days!

There are nine known kinds of pygmy squid.

Bigfin Squid

As their name suggests, bigfin squid are very big! They are among the largest squid in the ocean. Their long arms and **tentacles** reach lengths of up to 21 ft. (6.4 m)! This is around 20 times longer than their bodies.

Unlike other squid, bigfin squid have bends in their arms and tentacles, like elbows.

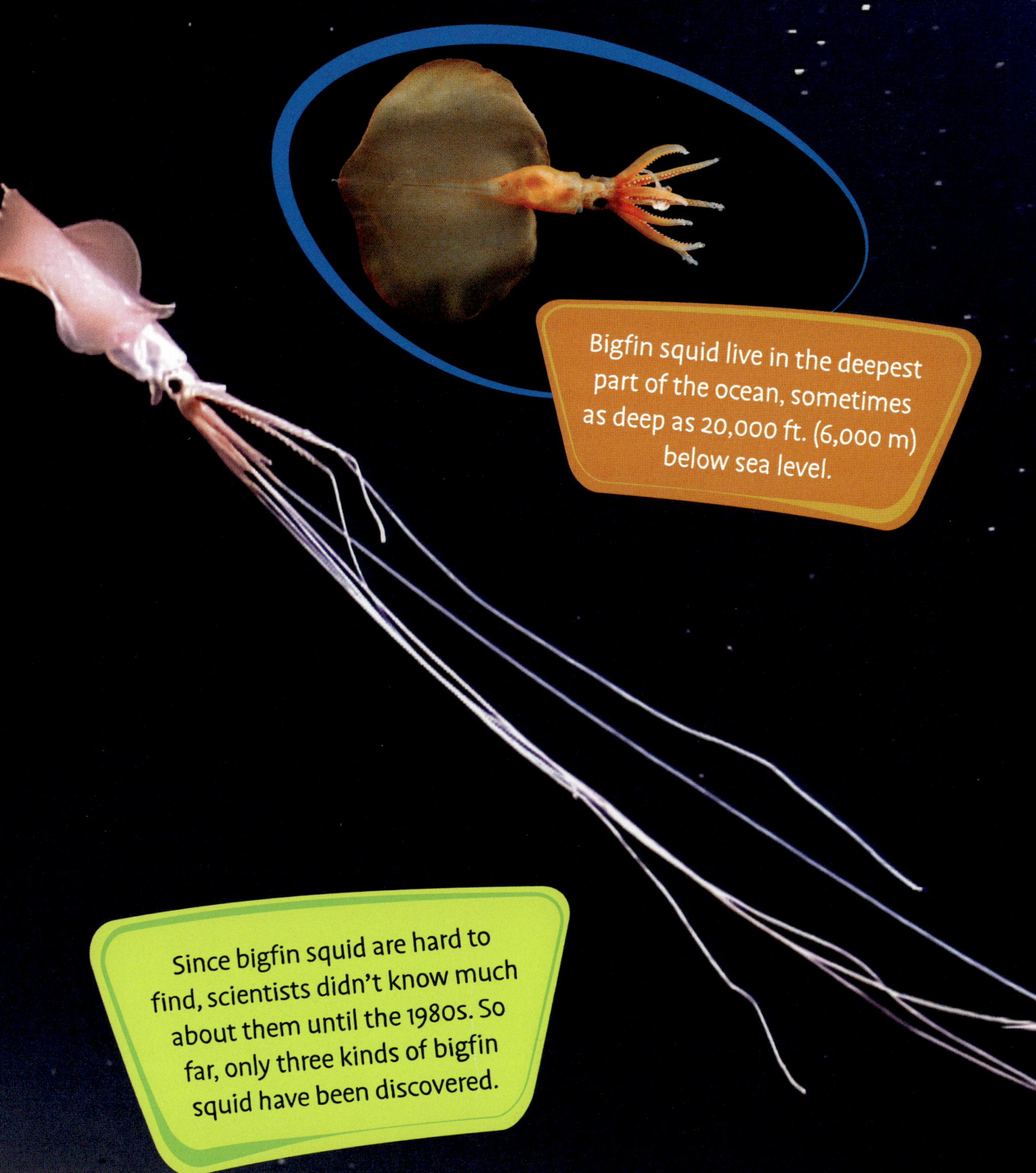

Bigfin squid live in the deepest part of the ocean, sometimes as deep as 20,000 ft. (6,000 m) below sea level.

Since bigfin squid are hard to find, scientists didn't know much about them until the 1980s. So far, only three kinds of bigfin squid have been discovered.

Weird and Wonderful

From flying squid to big-eared octopuses, the ocean is full of strange and surprising creatures. With their amazing shapes and clever ways to keep safe, octopuses and squid show us just how weird—and awesome—life underwater can be!

All octopuses and squid have blue blood!

The ghost octopus is one of the 300 or so kinds of octopuses around the world.
A ghost octopus
Octopuses and squid have lived on Earth for hundreds of millions of years. They were here long before people.

MEET AN UNDERWATER RESEARCHER

Alex Schnell is a marine biologist who works closely with octopuses. Her research focuses on the intelligence of these creatures. She has been able to prove that octopuses are a lot smarter than people used to think. They can even make plans!

Alex is the host of the TV show, *Secrets of the Octopus*.

GLOSSARY

coral reefs groups of rocklike structures formed from the skeletons of sea animals called coral polyps

disguise to hide oneself by looking like something else

female an animal that can lay eggs or give birth to young

male animals that cannot give birth to young

paralyze to cause something to be unable to move

prey animals that are hunted by other animals for food

tentacles long, thin body parts used by some animals for moving or stinging

venomous able to inject poison with bite or sting

INDEX

READ MORE

McDougal, Anna. *The Strange Life Cycle of an Octopus (Scientific American Investigates Life Cycles).* New York: Rosen Publishing, 2025.

Rose, Rachel. *Blue-Ringed Octopus (Danger Down Under).* Minneapolis: Bearport Publishing, 2024.

LEARN MORE ONLINE

1. Go to **FactSurfer.com** or scan the QR code below.
2. Enter "**Strange Dumbo Octopus**" into the search box.
3. Click on the cover of this book to see a list of websites.

About the Author

Rachel Rose lives in San Francisco. Her favorite thing to do there is to dip in the bay, where she swims with a lot of playful seals.